B

"You are holding in your hand a transformative guide that will change your life. Read every page, pause and take it in. I love this book. I couldn't put it down. I read it once and then I read it again and again. Deanna, thank you for sharing Brandon's miracle with the world."

— Simon T. Bailey
Author of *Shift Your Brilliance*

Brandon's friend Jake DeHoop,
was diagnosed with Leukemia
three years after Brandon and said,
"Brandon paved the road for us."

ISBN: 978-0-578-16995-8

Design: Performance Design Group
Printed in U.S.A. with soy inks

Speaking the
Language of Miracles®

You are powerful
What is inside of you
is much greater than any situation

I've lived through the first statement multiple times in ways I wouldn't wish on anyone.

When I was 15 years old, I was pronounced dead at the scene of a horrific motorcycle accident. My husband was once told he had six months to live. When my son was 10 years old, he was diagnosed with a rare form of Leukemia and was told he wouldn't be leaving the hospital.

None of those events ever came to pass, if it weren't for Speaking the Language of Miracles®. My walk has created in me an intense knowing that we have the ability to access the incredible power we are through our own language.

Your life can change in an instant
And you can intentionally change your life in an instant

The illness is not who I am®

Brandon pitching in
Little League

Brandon played football for
the Woodinville Falcons

Brandon played basketball
for the Woodinville Falcons

Brandon's Story

On Mother's Day, May 10th, 2005, my family and I celebrated my son, Brandon's, baseball tournament by playing a round of golf together. The following morning Brandon was not feeling well and instead of going to school, I followed an inner impulse to take him to the doctor. It was uncharacteristic for me to take him to the doctor because I typically observe my kids' cold or flu symptoms over a course of a couple of days before visiting the doctor's office. Keep in mind that Brandon was always the healthiest member of the family and rarely ever came down sick. He was known as an outstanding athlete playing baseball, football, basketball and he was an all-around team player.

The doctor thought Brandon had a common cold, however, he had seen several cases of mononucleosis recently and took the precaution of performing a blood test. Without that blood test my son would not be here today.

Two hours following the doctor visit I received a call from the doctor telling me to immediately rush Brandon to Children's Hospital due to an extremely low white blood cell count. Children's performed an emergency blood transfusion and upon his arrival the doctor told me Brandon was in a rare situation and he was diagnosed with an acute form of leukemia. The doctor shared he would not be leaving the hospital any time soon. Brandon's first question was, "Mom, does this mean I'm going to die?" I told him, "the illness is not who you are." And that is how our journey began.

My reason for sharing Speaking the Language of Miracles is to give back to Children's Hospital what they gave back to me — my son Brandon.

Miracles

Our Miracles Were in Our Language
What We Said We Created
Brandon's Miracles Were in His Language
What He Said He Created

We witnessed miracles every day for eight months. The first miracle was when the doctor asked to do a blood test on Brandon, when the doctor himself thought he had a common cold. Without that blood test my son would not have been alive the next day. The next miracle was when we got the blood test back in two hours. The doctor himself said it won't be back for two or three days, but I should keep him home if he doesn't feel good. After leaving the doctor's office, I asked Brandon if he wanted to go with me to take care of his sister's horse. Where his sister's horse was stabled it was a rural area, there was never any cell service. The next miracle, the phone rang and Brandon replied "that's weird, you never get cell service here." When I picked up the phone the doctor in a panic said: "Deanna it's an emergency, get Brandon to Children's hospital immediately, they are waiting for your arrival." Right then I hung up the phone and called my husband, but there was no cell service.

Just to let you know how serious Brandon's illness was, the nurses every hour on the hour for eight months would draw his blood to monitor his blood cells. From Brandon throwing up blood every day, sometimes buckets of blood. I forgot how many blood transfusions that he had! His fevers of 106 degrees would last sometimes for three days. Brandon's temperature would not go down until he declared out loud my temperature is 98.6 and visualized his temperature going down, and then it would. We would pray, but it would not change until he visualized and declared "my temperature is 98.6."

When his temperature climbed to 106 that's when he went into the intensive care unit.

The doctors shared how they were going to do a tracheotomy so he could breathe better. Right then I asked Brandon to focus on his temperature going down and that's when we saw it lowering. They did not do the tracheotomy, another miracle. We witnessed so much power in his word.

Miracles

Even though every day was a fight for his life, we never walked in the illness. Every day we reminded Brandon of who he is and talked of his future, never talking of his illness.

Brandon's doctor told us because of the type of Leukemia that Brandon had, he was going to need a bone marrow transplant. No one in the family was a match for Brandon. They put Brandon under anesthesia and went into his bone marrow to see what type he would need. Right before he went under he wrote out on paper: I have healthy blood cells throughout my body and I am a healthy child of God—over and over again on three pages. When the doctors came back to us, they shared that they had never seen this before with this type of Leukemia, that it was a miracle: "We are happy to share that your son does not need a bone marrow transplant. He has a higher chance of living." Tears of joy came running down our faces, thanking God.

When Brandon was able to write, he would write out his affirmations. That way we were walking in intent of his affirmation that day, we would see miracles take place. This is in your language, whatever you say you create. So, make it positive. All we did was let Brandon shine. By not bringing up the illness, we spoke Faith upon him. When all of his friends and our family would come up to me and say: "Deanna, I don't know if I can go into Brandon's room and not cry," all I did was remind everyone: the illness is not my son, remember who Brandon was before the illness. Then everyone was walking in the outcome of Brandon leaving the hospital and not walking in the illness. They remembered Brandon of who he was before he got sick.

Every Day that Brandon was Alive was a Miracle

The Situation is NOT Who I am.®
I am a Survivor.

This is Brandon's walk

I am with you all the way...

Learning the Language of Miracles™

Wellness

I am here to share how your language is one of the most powerful gifts that you have in this universe. Do not let your words limit you. Whatever you say, you create, so make the distinctions between what you are saying and what you are telling yourself. Is it positive 😊 or negative 🙁?

Remember the illness is not who you are and that you are the creator of your life. Create a life that you Love. Dream Big, don't let setbacks hold you down, continue to reinvent yourself. And remember our best days are ahead of us 😊.

If you have been told you have an illness, I hope this section of Wellness helps you. This was Brandon's walk and he proved to be a powerful being and a cancer survivor.

Parents

- Always focus on the positive outcome of your child being healthy, not the illness
- If you focus on the illness, it persists
- Never tell your child how sick they are, the illness is just a situation
- Interact the same way before your son or daughter got sick
- Even if your son/daughter has an illness, do not change the way you play and talk with him/her
- Replace the hospital room environment with home environment
- Bring the decorations from home to replicate what is familiar, hang family pictures on the walls, celebrations, drawings, school portraits, games, posters, toys, blankets, etc.
- Walk in the positive outcome of your child as a powerful spirit
- Communicate with your son or daughter as a healthy child with daily affirmations
- Talk with him/her in a positive way
- Tell him/her how successful they will be when they grow up
- Share with him/her how beautiful and healthy they are
- It's OK to spoil them, not pity them
- Surprise them with a home-cooked meal
- Start a scrapbook that they can add to
- Visualize the outcome of a healthy child
- Teach the Language of Miracles to family, friends, community members, hospital staff, and whoever your child sees
- Remind everyone that the illness is not your child, it's just the situation—it's not who they are
- Walk in the positive outcome and remember who they were before they had the illness
- Speak faith upon them
- Your child is not the illness
- Do not own the illness

Parents can share this concept with their children by talking to them about having goals and dreams. By doing this, you can help your child reinvent himself/herself. You can let your children know whenever bad situations occur that it is just a situation and not who they are. You can teach them to walk in their own spirit and not get caught up in the situations they might find themselves in.

Rejuvenation

It's very important to rejuvenate yourself through this adjustment. Keep yourself healthy with the right mindset.

I, myself, was exercising everyday at the hospital with a spin class and volunteered to help with animals, to rejuvenate myself, so when I walked into my son's room I could share what good things I did today. It's very important to fuel yourself and to walk in Faith with conviction of the outcome you want to achieve that day. It's important to keep yourself healthy while you're going through this adjustment, so you can be there for your son or daughter. I'm not saying it's easy. I remember going to the Faith Hill and Tim McGraw concert with a friend at Key Arena down the street from Children's hospital. The opening song was, "Live Like You Were Dying." Right then I broke down crying. But, after the concert, I was so pumped up I came right back to my son's room sharing how great the concert was. I remember how important it was for him to see me smile.

Think how you can pump yourself up to fight for your son or daughter. How can you rejuvenate yourself? What makes you happy?

- Taking walks
- Concerts
- Zoo
- Volunteer to help
- Garden
- Gym, Yoga, Pilates, Tai Chi, Spin Class
- Painting
- Horseback riding
- Sports Games

Rejuvenate Yourself to Stay Healthy

What Rejuvenates You?

**Walk in the
Outcome of your
Son and daughter
Leaving the Hospital**

Visualize your son and daughter healthy

**Speak wellness upon your child
You will have a better outcome when talking
About your child's future**

Remember:
The illness is not who I am®

**Fight and rebuke the illness
Make a stand for who you are
Believe in what you stand for
And stand for what you believe in**

Your Son or Daughter

- Think and walk in wellness and health
- The illness you have is just a situation
- The illness is not who you are; you are a powerful spirit
- Your goals and dreams don't stop because of your situation
- Remind yourself that you are not the illness
- Think of yourself as healthy
- Envision how you will look and feel after leaving the hospital

Record Your Goals and Dreams

- Where will you travel in the world?
- What will you be when you grow up?
- Will you be married? Have kids? How many?
- What will you study in school? Where will you go to college?
- What work do you want to do?

Brandon's goals and dreams at 10 years old

- Make-A-Wish® granted his wish and flew him to Memphis, Tennessee to play basketball with NBA player Mike Conley

Brandon's Affirmations

- I am going to be an NBA basketball player
- I am going to be married one time and have 2 kids
- When I leave the hospital, I'm going to bring my family to Atlantis

Brandon's affirmation and vision was going down the water slides at Atlantis in the Bahamas.

This is Brandon 8 months later:

**Brandon with Mike Conley, Jr.
of the Memphis Grizzlies**

MAKE·A·WISH®

Family members of the Child (patient):

- Live in the joy of the day (each day) by ONLY seeing your son or daughter for the possibility of who they say they are and not the illness
- Treat your child in the outcome of wellness
- Always walk in the positive outcome
- Start a rotation plan for people to visit
- Send progress updates on how your son or daughter is doing to family, friends, and community members

Brothers/Sisters:

- Be a support system and engage with your brother/sister
- Repeat affirmations with family members
- Share with your brother/sister everything that is going on with your life
- Support your brother/sister and family through this adjustment
- Always walk in the positive outcome and not negativity
- Visit your brother/sister and be with them as much as possible
- Play games
- Watch funny movies/funny TV shows
- Text them
- Skype with them
- Whatever activities you engaged in with your brother/sister before the illness, keep doing them to your best ability

Grandparents:

- Still talk and play with your grandchild in the same way as though they are visiting your home
- Examples from Brandon's Grandparents:
    - Playing catch in the hallway
    - Watching sports on TV
    - Encouraging laughter
    - Shooting baskets in his room (Brandon had a basketball hoop in his room)

Know:
You are an inspiration!

Your walk inspires others!

It takes pure courage to walk your walk!

Teachers:

- Make an effort to stay in communication as much as possible with the student
- Do not treat them differently just because they have an illness
- You may have to do simpler lessons, but never make the child feel like they are behind
- Instead, focus on being present in what the child is doing that day
- Try to keep the child up to date with not only class material but what is going on at the school as a whole and what they have to look forward to

Examples:

Tell them about school assemblies, school sports teams, clubs, changes to the school, things that happen with their peers or other teachers or staff (maybe there's a new lunch being served they can look forward to)

Coaches:

- Make an effort to stay in communication as much as possible with the child you coach
- Keep them up to speed on everything that's going on with the team
- When you visit, take play books and videos of games or practices to show them

Friends and Community Members:

- Support from friends and the community is immeasurable — a huge impact for your son or daughter
- The greater the effort visiting, the easier the adjustment is for your child
- Bring to the hospital things you would normally do at home:
    - Friends and community members brought movies, board games, card games, puzzles, etc., to the hospital
    - Community members brought homemade meals and treats to the hospital
    - Community members raised money by selling flowers and lemonade
    - Brandon's fifth grade teacher kept him up to date with school so he never fell behind and was not held back a grade
    - They made a banner that said "Brandon Rocks" with over a hundred classmates' and friends' signatures
    - They embroidered blankets and pillows
    - Classmates cut their hair in solidarity as they didn't want Brandon to feel alone. It put them in the same place with Brandon.

Friends of Brandon shaved their heads to support him.

Reminding You
You are a healthy child of God

God is in your DNA
You are the CREATOR of your life

You are powerful
What is inside of you
is much greater than the illness

Life

- Speaking the Language of Miracles ignites the flame within you.
- The flame represents God's spirit. My belief is that everyone has God's spirit within themselves.
- Ask yourself: Is your heart open to the gifts that are inside of you? Watch the miracle take place.
- With Speaking the Language of Miracles, you can make the distinctions if you are using your gifts.
- Teach Speaking the Language of Miracles to family, friends, community members and whomever you encounter.
- Remind everyone that the situation they are dealing with or encounter does not change who they are as an individual. Walk in the positive outcome of who you are.

Daily Affirmations so they can see a "Healthy Reflection"

Daily Affirmations:

- I am a healthy child of God
- I am receiving all great blessings today
- I am a powerful spirit
- I am walking in joy
- I am happy
- I am beautiful
- I am loving
- I am giving
- I am forgiving
- I am caring
- I am successful
- I am a major contribution to my family, friends and community
- I am of my word
- I am trusting
- I am loyal
- I am a leader
- I am powerful
- I am walking in financial abundance
- I am a survivor

Faith

Within your own individual faith, it's important to speak with conviction of the outcome you want to achieve.

Believe in what you pray for

Brandon would pray as if his prayers were already answered.

Thank you God, I am a healthy child of God.

Thank you God, I am receiving all great blessings today.

Thank you God, I have healthy blood cells throughout my entire body.

We turned everything over to God and saw miracles every day.

Thank you God

The illness is not who I am®

Encouragement for Faith

What is faith? The best description comes from the Bible – the resource for building faith.

"Faith is the confidence that what we hope for will actually happen; it gives us assurance about things we cannot see." — *Hebrews 11:1*

"I tell you the truth, if you have faith even as small as a mustard seed, you could say to this mountain, Move from here to there, and it would move. Nothing would be impossible." — *Matthew 17:20*

But there are times when our faith comes under incredible seasons of testing. Maybe you have found yourself wrestling with doubt, fear and unbelief in a circumstance beyond your control. It's critical that at these times when you are at your weakest and most faithless point that you be mindful of what you say because your words are like seeds. Once spoken out into your world, in time your words will bring a harvest. So speak your desired outcome and declare that your dreams for the future will come to reality, no matter what you see around you.

Are you wrestling with a situation that is challenging your faith on every side?

What is your dream? What is the "Mountain" standing in your way?

Speaking the Language of Miracles is here to help you through this time in your life, to help you take hold of your God-given promises. Believe and declare your dreams come true. Here are some declarations that will help you get started and feel free to personalize these statements by inserting your name or a loved-one's name wherever it is appropriate:

The illness is not who you are and it is trespassing on God's property! (You!)

I am not who people say I am (sick, poor, dying, unable, etc.) I am who God says I am.

God says I am more than victorious through Him who loves me.

God says that greater is He that is in me.

My son and I are here to help you with your fight.

This is the fight of your life
We believe in you
Your gifts are inside of you

This was our fight and Brandon and I are here to share our Gifts, because we know you have the same gifts within you.

We are reminding you that the illness is NOT who you are

Brandon's nurse, Stacy

Brandon 8 years later on the Woodinville
High School Golf Team

Brandon's Miracle:

Brandon did not allow his illness to affect his goals and dreams he had for the future. He proved to be a powerful being and a cancer survivor.

Today my son is cancer free. This would have never been possible without the help and support from family members, friends, coaches, teachers, and our whole community. I am here today to share Brandon's story and share with people how influential Speaking the Language of Miracles can be for a child or loved one dealing with an illness.

Dreams Come True

Brandon 10 years later, holding Christine, sharing their life together.

Whatever You Think, You Will Create

Live a Life You Love

I am a Survivor

Brandon and Christine

Learning the Language of Miracles

You can apply this mindset in every part of your life to walk in a better outcome

Learning the Language of Miracles

How to Apply Language of Miracles to Your Life™

Kids are our Future

Each and every one of us makes a ripple effect in the world. What's the ripple effect that you want to create?

Dream Big
You are the World

Create a Life you Love

It's so easy to make the right choices in everything we do, when we look at the outcome, if it's positive 😊 or negative 🙁.

Kids are our Future

Morals = Treat people the same as you would want done unto you. Look at the outcome, is it positive 😊 or negative 🙁?

Values = Faith Foundation within your own individual faith. Look at the outcome, is it positive 😊 or negative 🙁 ?

Integrity = Being a person of your word, Being honest and fair. Look at the outcome, is it positive 😊 or negative 🙁?

Accountability = Being responsible for your actions, Saying you're sorry. Look at the outcome, is it positive 😊 or negative 🙁?

Patience = Not walking in the situation. Look at the outcome, is it positive 😊 or negative 🙁?

Gratitude = When you're thankful for everyone and everything in your life, Look at the outcome, is it positive 😊 or negative 🙁 ?

Love = To give love and receive love, what's the outcome?

Respect = Respecting others, what's the outcome?

Trust = Walking in faith, what's the outcome?

Caring = Look at the outcome, is it positive 😊 or negative 🙁?

Giving = Look at the outcome to giving.

Sharing = Look at the outcome to sharing.

Distinctions = Look at the outcome to everything we do.

Situations

Always make distinctions of what the situation is:

Media, Bad News, Drama, Gossip, Divorce, Death, Illness, Jealousy, Hate, He said-She said, Liar liar pants on fire.

Situations are always negative, they rob us of who we are! We are much greater than any situation. People who create drama are joy stealers. Never partake in the situation. Instead, have empathy for that person that is going through a hard time. Remind them the situation is not who they are. Surround yourself with positive, happy, creative, successful people who Dream Big. When you hang out with successful people, it's contagious 😊.

The positive things we say is what we attract back to us.

Listen to your words of what you are saying, is it positive 😊 or negative 🙁? The situation is the enemy in many forms. The enemy wants you to walk in the situation. The enemy wants you to be powerless. The enemy wants you to walk in sickness, broken relationships, failing businesses and recessions. The enemy does not want you to walk in solutions. The enemy doesn't want you to walk in the outcome of success. The enemy doesn't want you to walk in your God-given gifts. But we are victorious and we will conquer the situation. The enemy will always want us to stay in the situation.

If you have identified that you are always sharing negative situations, the good news is: it's not who you are. You can have the clarity to make the choice to change that mindset. And, guess how long it takes to make that change?

In an Instant

Surround yourself with positive people and watch your Dreams become a reality.

The Situation is Not Who You Are!

Create world peace with
Speaking the Language of Miracles

Imagine what the world would look like
with world peace

The situation is our enemy,
NOT each other

We are the World

All it takes is a mindset to have world peace. Make the Distinction that the situation is our enemy and not each other.

What is your World Vision?

I "choose" to be pro life. No more wars. All it takes is one person, one voice to unite.

What is the outcome of no more wars?

Instead of spending trillions of dollars to destroy our planet and each other, we can take that money and save our planet and create a better world.

We have the power, technology and language to create a better world.

Walk here on earth as you would in heaven.

Create your world as if it was in heaven.

You are
The
Creator
of
Your
Life

Create
A
Life
You
Love

Affirmations

Help your vision become real.
What are your Goals and Dreams?

I am: _____

I am creating: _____

I enjoy: _____

I am: _____

I am creating: _____

I enjoy: _____

I am: _____

I am creating: _____

I enjoy: _____

I am: _____

I am creating: _____

I enjoy: _____

Dream Big

Anything you think you can create.

What will you be when you grow up?

_____

_____

_____

_____

What do you have envisioned for your future?

_____

_____

_____

_____

How will you change the world?

_____

_____

_____

How will you make the world a better place?

_____

_____

_____

Everything that we were taught and instilled in us when we were little, is what we use today. Some of us have been derailed because of our situations, and have created stories that we hide behind. I truly want you to know how beautiful you are. And, what is inside of you is much more powerful than any situation. God created you Perfect and Beautiful in every way.

Remember:
The situation is NOT who you are!

Choices

Every choice you make causes a ripple effect in everything you do. No matter how big or small know what your gifts are, and know how powerful you are, listen to your language. Do you choose to make your choices positive or negative?

It's easy making the right choices, when you look at the outcome of what you want to achieve, is it:

Positive or Negative

You can make your dreams come true with the right choices.

Staying Focused on Creating Your Dreams is Walking In The Language Of Miracles

By walking in the Language of Miracles you make choices that create opportunities for you to be successful. It's never too early and it's never too late to start making the right choices.

The choices that you make from first grade through high school graduation matter towards what you envision achieving after high school. Let's say that your goal is to attend a 4-year university after high school. Choosing to place such high importance on your school work from elementary school through high school gives you an edge when it comes time to apply to a university.

My daughter, Taylor, "walked in the outcome" and graduated from the University of Washington. She then went on to land her dream job in Los Angeles to create a life she loves.

It's up to you to decide where you want to go and what you want to do, what choices will help you and which ones will hinder you.

Tailor These Choices to Your Own Ambitions:

Being goal-minded works

Find something you love to do:
- Focus on obtaining your dream job 5, 10 and 20 years or further down the road
- What choices will elevate you towards landing that job?

Create long-term goals
Examples:
- If you're in high school, in what industry of work do you want to be in after college?
- If you're in college, what type of boss do you want to be one day?
- If you're in your first job, what do you want to create for the company that elevates the entire organization to a higher level?
- If you were to be alive at the reading of your eulogy, what do you want someone to write and say about you?

If you don't know what you love to do yet, create short-term obtainable goals.
This will aid in finding something you're passionate about and at the same time discover what you want in life
Examples:
- Landing a job interview
- Making a sports team
- Improving your academic performance
- Learning new skills

Surround yourself with leaders

Find mentors you look up to from whom you can learn
- Teachers, counselors, work colleagues, bosses, family members
- Make it a point to stay in contact with people who inspire you or to whom you look up to
  - Schedule a coffee or lunch
  - Ask them for advice, learn from the experiences that they share with you
  - Always have a list of at least 5 topics/questions to discuss with your leaders/mentors
- If you don't have many physical mentors:
  - Find authors or speakers who you can read and listen to (TED talks, podcasts, autobiographies, community seminars)

Practice makes perfect

- Practice pushing yourself forward, constantly finding new opportunities to take ahold of and follow through on them
- Practice finding a routine that will benefit your life and future (ask a mentor or read about successful peoples' daily routines, fine-tune what you learn from them and create your own routine)
  - Some people wake up and go for a run first thing
  - Some drink a cup of hot water while reading the newspaper
- Practice finding as many work experiences as possible from an early age
- Practice writing out everything
  - Keep a journal or write in your phone "notes" section
    - Goal setting not just on a yearly basis but more frequently
    - Write everything down (ideas that come to mind, accomplishments you envision yourself achieving)
- Practice communicating with multiple personalities and different types of people of different backgrounds
- Practice being a go-getter rather than waiting to be asked to do something
- Practice visualization
  - While stating an affirmation, envision what that affirmation looks like
  - Examples:
    - Holding a college acceptance letter
      - What will you study? Where you will live on campus? How will it feel?
    - Receiving a job offer
      - How will you respond? What will they offer you exactly? How will you accept?
    - Delivering a presentation
      - Who will be in the room? To whom will you direct your attention while speaking? What questions will you answer?

You are Amazing!

Walk in your gifts that are in you.

**Speaking The
Language of Miracles
In Business**

Whatever You Think You Create

Whatever your Mindset is, it sets the Foundation for your Business Success

To walk in the positive outcome you need to remember one thing:

The situation is NOT who you are.®

All it takes is

Distinctions

of the right language to attract what you want in your business.

Walking in Success

Remember:
The Situation is NOT who you are.

The Situation Is NOT Who I Am

In 2008, my dog grooming business was very successful. I was getting new referrals every day from existing clients who would give out my name and number. I never advertised my business. It was all by word of mouth. When my friends and other business owners would ask me how I was doing so well in this recession, I would reply back and say: The recession is NOT who I am. It's just a situation!!! I have a mindset that my business is thriving, I walk in the outcome everyday of what I want to achieve and be my very best.

Affirmations every morning help me walk in intent of what I want to achieve this day and every day.

Before I get up in the morning I say my affirmations in bed. My first one is:

- I am receiving all great blessings today
  (Doesn't that feel good? Starts my day off great!)
- I am a contribution to my clients
- I love my work
- I love my clients
- I am walking in financial abundance
- I have new clients every day
- I am successful
- I am the greatest
- I am happy

And because I made a choice to begin my day with such a great start, I receive all great blessings throughout the day. I walk in intent of my affirmations ☺. I give my thanks to God to be my very best, thank Him throughout my day, and I am very grateful and thankful for the clients I have.

Distinctions

My paradise is in front of me every day. It's just that I have the clarity to see I'm creating it.

And now so do you, all it takes is:

Clarity = Making distinctions

Choices = Positive or negative? When you look at the outcome of what you want to achieve, if it's positive or negative, it's easy to make the right choices.

Accountability = Own your life, own your mistakes, do not blame others.

Integrity = Trust; be someone of your word. Without your word, you're nothing. Follow up with what you say.

Look at the outcome of following up with your word, and then look at the outcome of NOT following up with your word.

To be successful in business, you need to trust the person you're doing business with. Your language is everything. When you follow up with your word, people can trust you.

This Is How To Have A Healthier Mindset

Put the situation on the wall, step back and watch yourself get inspired. The situation is Not who you are.

Walk, Talk in Solutions

- Make Distinctions
- Reinvent
- Take Action
- Implement
- Have a Positive Mindset

Choices

It's easy making the right choices when you look at the outcome that you want to achieve. Make distinctions, is it **positive** or **negative**?

Make Distinctions

What didn't work? Move forward.

Make distinctions. What is working?

Have the clarity to know when you're walking and talking in the situation.

That's Defeat

Nothing can change when you're walking and talking in the situation.

Have the clarity to know that it's a negative. We don't have the time to walk in the situation. This is the Internet world. Everything happens in an instant. Speaking the Language of Miracles is the fastest way out of the situation. Greatness is in our DNA.

Distinctions within Real Estate

When you say there is a shortage of homes for sale to a co-worker or client, what are you attracting back to you? What's the outcome?

Instead

When you say this is a great time to buy and sell to a co-worker, client, and everyone else — what are you attracting back to you?

What's the outcome to this mindset?
All it takes is a mind shift to have the clarity of what your language is around you to attract what you want.

Choices and Distinctions

We will have another recession in the future, but with this mindset we will have a better outcome with everything we do.

Whatever you think, you will create. Have you ever been inspired by someone and said, "I wish I could do that" or "I wish I could make as much as that person", but make excuses why you can't? It's because these individuals love what they are doing. Make the right choice — are you in the right job and career?

Just know there isn't anything you can't have today. What is your self talk? The only thing stopping you is yourself. If there's anything you don't like in your life, you need to look in the mirror. You have attracted everything that you have today: good and bad . . . hopefully more good.

What I'm trying to identify with you is that all the good things you have in your life today is from a positive mindset inside of you that I want you to identify. You didn't achieve these great things in your life with a negative mindset. My wish for you is to quadruple your positive mindset and to create a life that you love, and to remind you of who you are. You are victorious. You are the creator of your life, Dream Big!

We all have Free Will to make the choices in our lives.

What is the outcome of your choices that you are making?

You are the Winning Formula

So often we choose to walk in the situation and when we do, we don't see who we are. The situation robs us of our God-given unique gifts of who we are.

You are much more Powerful than any Situation.

Choose to apply your gifts that are inside of you, to walk and talk in Solutions. Your gifts overcome any situation. All you need is the mindset to make the distinction to choose to walk in solutions.

Office Meetings   Leadership Meetings
Strategy Meetings   Board Meetings

When you're in your group meetings, do you leave just talking about the problems, or do you leave feeling inspired, energized and walking and talking in Solutions?

You are the Winning Formula!

Speaking The Language Of Miracles

*To be successful in Life,
in Wellness, in Relationships and in Business, you
Need to continue to reinvent yourself.*

Speaking the Language of Miracles is the most powerful
way to reinvent yourself and to walk in success in
everything you do.

John L. Scott Testimonial

Applying Speaking the Language of Miracles in Business at John L. Scott Real Estate

Chairman and CEO: J. Lennox Scott

J. Lennox Scott is a third generation Chairman and CEO of John L. Scott Real Estate, which was founded by his grandfather in Seattle in 1931. From the beginning, John L. Scott's success has been from its focus on each individual client.

Lennox is a three-time recipient of *Realtor* Magazine's 25 Most Influential People in Real Estate in the nation. Lennox serves on the National Association of Realtors' Board of Directors and Real Estate Services Advisory Group as well as the Realtor® University Research Policy and Advisory Committee.

John L. Scott has over 110 offices with more than 2,900 sales associates in the states of Washington, Oregon and Idaho. In 2015, John L. Scott will close 34,000 transactions for over 10 billion dollars in sales volume.

I, Lennox, met Deanna on December 13, 2008. I could tell instantly that she was a powerful spirit. About a month after first meeting her, I asked how she was so successful during the economic collapse that our country was going through. That's when she said "the recession is not who I am." Deanna shared she does not listen to the news media or negative talk; "I only walk in the outcome of what I want to achieve."

That's when I asked her if I could use her concepts, her affirmations in my business. I always used affirmations but her spirit, her walk, her speaking, resonated with me. It psychologically and emotionally took me to a higher state of being.

The situation is NOT who you are

The Great Recession

In the year 2007, the housing market started to deteriorate. Then in year 2008, it accelerated downward to substantially lower sales activity and prices. It would have been easy to make the statement that this is a terrible housing market and then just wallow in it.

I have always been a positive person, but then I met Deanna and she helped elevate my spirit through her approach in creating distinctions and, more importantly, being relentlessly focused on the positive outcome.

Distinction: "The recession is not who I am"

Positive Outcome: "I am successful, I am a major contribution to my clients, I am Walking in Abundance."

Positive Mind Set is at the core of success. It's who you are. Your higher purpose is helping your clients.

Your mindset psychologically is the inspiration that helps you create personal motivation to move forward to accomplish, to provide a higher level of service, and to walk in joy within your work.

As a business, we are excelling in greater heights at this time with Speaking the Language of Miracles but there always seems to be a recession every 10 years. Although the next one will be shorter in duration than the Great Recession, we are already prepared for the situation. We will walk in success. We will walk in the positive outcome.

Current example:

Shortage of inventory of homes for sale.

Instead of accepting this as fact and placing yourself as a victim, what are you going to do about it?

That's where Positive Affirmations come into play.

I find Homeowners who want to sell their home. This is what I state each day on the way to work. So, by the time I get into the office I am in action.

Instead of dwelling in the situation, walk in the outcome of what you want to achieve.

Write up the situation in a few words, printing it on a pieces of paper and tape it to a wall; step back and take a look. Then the next important step:

What are you going to do about it?

What is the positive outcome that you want?

Focus on solutions to handle and overcome the situation, then detail out your action steps to accomplish this.

Personal Business Affirmations

- I am a Powerful Spirit
- I am a major contribution to my Clients
- I am walking in abundance in my Career
- I am Financially Successful
- I am walking in the Positive Outcome

Think Big – Dream Bigger

Fully express yourself; continually go through a renewal of spirit.

We have always done Strategic Planning and Business Plans at work which is a form of Thinking Big. But speaking the Language of Miracles has brought it alive and keeps our momentum moving forward by making declarations of your service and personal commitments.

When I first met Deanna, after hearing her language and concepts, I made the statement:

"I can see I'm not thinking big enough"

We have been applying **Speaking the Language of Miracles** to walk in success in everything we do.

It Takes Courage to Walk in Solutions

What are Your Solutions

What is Speaking the
Language of Miracles in Business?

Not to walk in the situation.

The situation is not who you are. Whatever you talk about, it will persist and grow. So, that is why you want to talk in and about solutions. Implement and take action to your solutions, write out your solutions. Make distinctions as to what is working in your company. Stop talking about what's not working. That is attracting negative energy back to you. It's impossible to walk in solutions when you are walking in the situation.

Stop talking about other companies, it's not greener on the other side. The green is inside of you. You are the winning formula.

When you walk in this mindset, you see your unique gifts and your talents flow out of you. You see yourself inspired, Speaking the Language of Miracles brings out your Higher Purpose.

All because you choose not to walk in the situation.

Language of Miracles
is the
Winning Formula

Learn How to use
Language of Miracles in
Relationships

Marriage

My husband Lennox and I both walk in success by Speaking the Language of Miracles in every aspect of our lives. We put God first in everything we do and continuously walk in the outcome.

We reinvent ourselves through our marriage, our children, business, and our goals and dreams by making distinctions. This means that when certain situations arise, good or bad, we separate them from who we are as individuals. We say to ourselves, "That is not who I am, it is just a situation." By taking this approach, we are able to walk in who we are and not in the situation. We say our affirmations every morning before getting out of bed. We walk in love every day with each other and give thanks for all our blessings. When we complete one goal or dream, we make new ones because whatever you think and declare, you will create. So dream big and think positive because your best days are ahead of you. All it takes is a mindset for you to live and create a life you love.

When situations occur, we make the distinctions of what the situation is and walk in our desired outcome. By doing so you can walk in success within your business, relationships, wellness and your overall life. You cannot change things if you are walking in the situation. Instead, you can see change take place by taking yourself out of the situation and, by doing so, great things will happen!

Reinvent Yourself

An important aspect of Speaking the Language of Miracles is to reinvent yourself. By doing so, you create healthy relationships with your spouse, children, family members and friends.

I truly believe that by applying Speaking the Language of Miracles in your own life, you are able to have a better outcome in everything you do. All of this starts with the powerful statement:

Remember, "The situation is NOT who I am"

You are the Creator of Your Life

Remember: You are the CREATOR of your life

Whatever you think you will Create

You cannot have a future if you are living in past pain, whether in Relationships, Business or Life.

I'm reminding you, you are the creator of your life. What is in your DNA is much greater than any situation. Picture yourself on a white canvas. What will you create? Don't allow the situation on your canvas! It makes it impossible to move forward in life. Our situations do not serve us; we must let them go! And only keep the joy, laughter, and love on our canvas. What does your canvas look like? And we must always remember:

The situation is NOT who we are!

You are meant to have abundance in every part of your life. The only thing stopping you is yourself. Whatever you think, you will create.

So dream big and think positive!

"I am the greatest!"
Muhammad Ali

How to Apply Language of Miracles in Sports

When you are playing sports ask yourself, are you playing on the court full out or just on the sidelines, watching everyone else? I am here to share with you that your life is not a dress rehearsal. Always play on the court full out, with everything you do; every play is a new beginning. Always play as if it is your last game. Do not be on the sidelines with your life. Claim it, own it, and declare aloud "I am the greatest", just like Muhammad Ali.

1. What are your verbal affirmations that you are telling yourself? Are you declaring, owning, and walking in who you are?

2. Make your list and say them out loud every day before you get out of bed.

It makes a difference. You start walking with conviction and with the intent of who you are. That is when you see the change take place.

Affirmation Examples:

- I am receiving all great blessings today
- I am powerful
- I am healthy
- I am strong
- I am patient
- I am the greatest
- I am loyal
- I am a great team player
- I am a leader
- I am full of energy

Have a mental image of the outcome to every play.

Watch videos of yourself in action to see if your mind and body are in alignment with what you want to achieve.

- Every athlete's "I am" is different.
- Write out affirmations specific to you and declare your list of affirmations out loud everyday when you get out of bed, before a game, with your team, and anywhere else you can.
- Examples of specific athlete affirmations:
  I am the greatest football, baseball, golf, basketball, hockey, soccer, horseback, rugby, etc.… player or performer.

Make Peace

Forgiveness

To forgive, to be grateful, and to extend gratitude are very important parts of your life. You can watch your life transform with forgiveness, gratefulness, and with the expression of gratitude.

Make distinctions regarding the "outcome" of forgiveness and then make the distinctions regarding "not" forgiving. What is the outcome?

Forgiveness does not mean having to continue to put yourself in that place of hurt. Forgiveness is a part of going forward so you do not remain hurt. You cannot have a future if you are living in past pain.

Gratitude

Declare out loud every day what you are thankful for.

Remember, the situation is NOT who you are.

God says I am Victorious

How to Apply Language of Miracles To your Life Transitions

Speaking the Language of Miracles helps you walk in your spirit of who you are.

All the love, energy and gifts that are inside of you – you take with you to your next life.

Distinctions

Imagine walking in the situation, taking illness, baggage, anger, and past pain to your next life transition; that would be living in hell.

Release all past pain. You don't want to take your baggage with you into your next life or through your transition.

Imagine how good it feels leaving all baggage behind you and only walking in your Spirit, Love, and Joy of who you are; that's walking in heaven.

Speaking the Language of Miracles reminds you of who you are.

Speaking the Language of Miracles®

When you apply this to every part of your life: "The situation is not who you are," you allow your God-given gifts that are inside of you to rise up and walk in Victory. By not walking in the situation you automatically walk in the outcome of what you want to achieve.

Again: "The situation is not who you are"

God says I am victorious through Him who loves me.

Share with friends, family, coworkers, and your entire community how
Speaking The Language of Miracles can help add to their lives.

Order a copy for your loved ones at:
SpeakingTheLanguageOfMiracles.com

And start creating a life you love.

Part of the proceeds from each book sale goes directly to support
Children's Hospitals.
(With no Administrative Overhead)